Designed by Flowerpot Press
www.FlowerpotPress.com
CHC-0909-0509
ISBN: 978-1-4867-1862-7
Made in China/Fabriqué en Chine

Copyright © 2020 Flowerpot Press,
a Division of Flowerpot Children's Press, Inc., Oakville,
ON, Canada and Kamalu LLC, Franklin, TN, U.S.A.

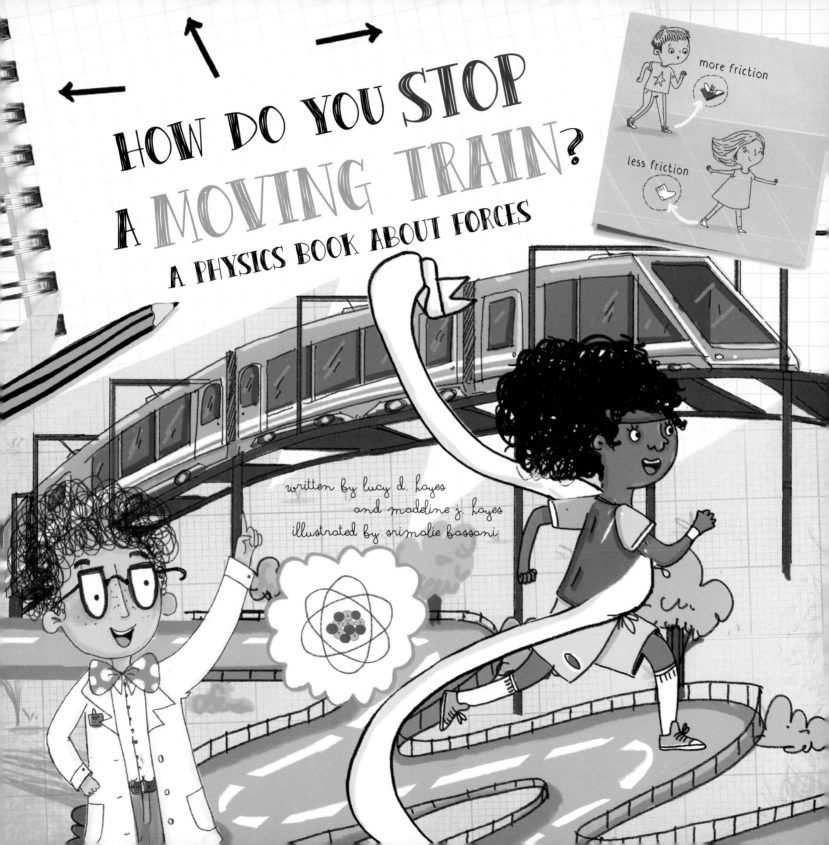

HOW DO YOU STOP A MOVING TRAIN?

A PHYSICS BOOK ABOUT FORCES

written by lucy d. hayes
and madeline j. hayes
illustrated by srimalie bassani

more friction

less friction

How do cars move? How do trains stop? How do airplanes fly? Physics! Physics is the science of movement. Physics can explain how elbows and knees bend the way they do, how wheels go 'round, and how balls bounce. Physics can be simple or complex. Learning physics can help you become an engineer, a doctor, an astronaut, or just a smarter kid!

5 miles

10 miles

SCHOOL

SCHOOL

The world's largest measuring tape?!?! No way!

When you move from one place to another, you can describe it in two ways—there is the distance you traveled and there is the displacement, which is from where you started to where you end up.

When measuring distance we measure all the ground we cover as we move from one place to another. In the picture, the longest distance is the route the bus takes (yellow). It is the longest because it has to stop at all the different neighborhoods before going to the school.

The second longest distance is the route a car would take to school (pink). This route is slightly longer than the direct route because you follow the road.

The shortest distance is the direct route (green). Even though it is the fastest, you can't go that way because there are other houses and things in the way.

Even though all three of these routes are different distances, the displacement for all of them is the same because no matter what, you always start at your home and end at the school.

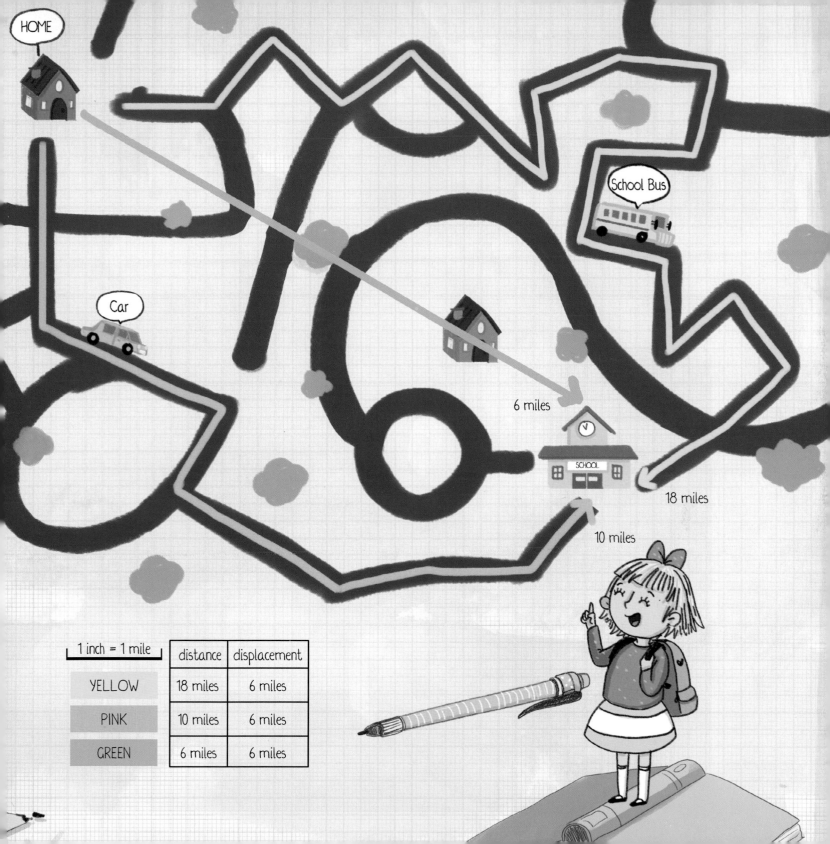

How do you know if you are the fastest kid in your school?
Do you challenge everyone to a race?

Race everyone in your school?!?! Well you could, but that would take a LONG time!

You could also compare how fast you all are without having to race. The measure of how fast something moves is called speed.

You can figure out your speed by taking the entire distance you covered from start to finish and dividing it by the total time it takes you to run that distance.

You can find your velocity by finding your speed and then adding in the direction you were running. When you think about speed in a specific direction, you're thinking about velocity.

SPEED, DISTANCE, TIME

$$speed = \frac{distance}{time}$$

For example, if you run 8 miles and it takes you 2 hours, you can calculate your speed in miles per hour (MPH) by dividing your distance by the time it took you to run that distance.

distance: 8 miles
time: 2 hours
$$\text{speed} = \frac{8 \text{ miles}}{2 \text{ hours}} = 4 \text{ MPH}$$

If you want to know your velocity, you would simply calculate your speed and then add in the direction you were running. For example, if you were running northwest in the example above, then your velocity would be 4 MPH northwest.

How do race cars speed up so fast?
Do they have a giant give them a big push at the beginning of the race?

A giant?!?! No way!

Cars can speed up and slow down all on their own.
They simply adjust their acceleration!

ACCELERATION FORMULA

$$\text{Acceleration} = \frac{\text{final velocity} - \text{initial velocity}}{\text{final time} - \text{initial time}}$$

Acceleration is the measure of how much your velocity changes divided by how much time it takes for it to change. For example, if you are in a stopped car, the car's velocity is 0 MPH. If the car takes 60 seconds to speed up from 0 MPH to 90 MPH, then to find the acceleration, you subtract the car's final velocity by its initial velocity and divide that by the time it takes to get to the final velocity.

$$\frac{90 \text{ MPH} - 0 \text{ MPH}}{60 \text{ seconds} - 0 \text{ seconds}} = 1.5 \text{ MPH per second}$$

That means, that on average, every second that passes, the car is going 1.5 MPH faster until it reaches 90 MPH.

You can do the same calculation if the car is slowing down.

$$\frac{0 \text{ MPH} - 90 \text{ MPH}}{0 \text{ seconds} - 60 \text{ seconds}} = -1.5 \text{ MPH per second}$$

That means, that on average, every second that passes, the car is going 1.5 MPH slower until it reaches 0 MPH.

How do you get your pizza from your dinner plate into your mouth?
Do you use mind control?

Mind control?!?! No way!
You're really smart, but that can't be possible.

While the pizza is at rest on the plate, a physical action has to be taken on the pizza in order for it to make its way up to your mouth. This physical action is called a force. A force is a push or pull exerted on an object that causes a change in that object's motion. There are many different ways forces cause changes in motion. Forces can cause an object to speed up, slow down, turn, start, or stop its motion. In the case of the pizza, your hand exerts a force on the pizza, pulling it up from rest, and speeds it up toward your mouth. Then after you take a bite, your hand pulls the pizza back down to the plate.

$$F = m \times a$$

force mass acceleration

If the mass is the same then more force equals more acceleration.

To calculate how much force it would take to pick up your pizza, you can multiply the pizza's mass times its acceleration. This is the same as Newton's second law of motion. You'll learn more about Newton's laws later on in this book!

push

pull

How do you stop a moving train?
Do you wait for a superhero to soar down and use their super strength?

A superhero?!?! No way! You don't need a superhero to stop a train.

EXAMPLES OF FRICTION

more friction

less friction

Wheel sliding along track

A train can stop on its own using its brakes. Train brakes work to stop the train using something called friction. Friction is a force that happens when two objects rub against each other. When a train uses its brakes, the brakes create friction between the wheels and the tracks to slow down the train until it stops.

Some surfaces have more friction than others. This is why you can slip across a floor easily in your socks but not as easily in your shoes. There is less friction between your socks and the floor than there is between the soles of your shoes and the floor.

Friction can heat things up!

rub your hands together

FORCES

How do astronauts float in outer space?
Do they drink a magical potion that helps them float around?

A magic potion?!?! No way! Although science is so cool that sometimes it does seem like magic!

Astronauts float in space because they feel so little gravity. Gravity is a force objects have on each other that helps hold them together.

floating potion

The gravitational effect that one object has on another depends on the size of the two objects and the distance between them. More distance means less gravity. Larger objects mean more gravity. For example, even though we don't really feel it, the gravity on Earth is what keeps us from floating into space. At the Space Station, astronauts are far enough away from Earth that they don't feel the force of Earth's gravity as much which is why they can float. This is also why a person can jump higher on the surface of the moon than they can on Earth, because Earth is larger than the moon and has a stronger gravitational pull.

NEWTON'S LAWS OF MOTION

Sir Isaac Newton is known as one of the most important and influential scientists in history. Newton's laws of motion laid a lot of the groundwork for how we learn math and science today, and they explain how forces work to move objects. Learn about Newton's laws to help you understand forces.

❶ THE LAW OF INERTIA

An object at rest will stay at rest and an object in motion will stay in motion unless acted on by an unbalanced force. This means that objects won't move or stop moving until they encounter some sort of force. For example, a soccer ball won't move until you kick it, but when you do, it won't stop moving until either another object or person touches it or until friction, gravity, and air resistance make it slow down and stop.

❷ FORCE EQUALS MASS TIMES ACCELERATION

The acceleration of an object created by a force is related to the amount of force and the mass of the object. This means that more force is required to move an object that has more mass than an object that has less mass. For example, when you go bowling with your friends, you will notice that it is easier to roll a four-pound bowling ball than a ten-pound bowling ball. This is because a ten-pound bowling ball has more mass and requires more force to send it down the lane than a four-pound bowling ball does.

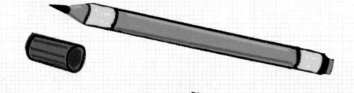

❸ FORCES COME IN PAIRS

For every action there is an equal and opposite reaction. For example, if you are jumping on a trampoline, your legs are applying force to the trampoline when you squat down to begin your jump. At the same time, the trampoline is applying force onto your feet, which is then what allows you to jump into the air. Two forces!

To learn even more about physics, try out some of these friction and gravity experiments at home. Be sure to ask for an adult's help before attempting these experiments.

PALM FRICTION EXPERIMENT
Use your hands to make friction.

Try it out:
1. Bring your hands together so that your palms are touching.
2. Rub your palms together back and forth as fast as you can.
3. When you feel your hands begin to warm up, that means the friction between your palms is creating heat.

rub your hands together

RICE AND PENCIL EXPERIMENT
Lift a bottle of rice using just a pencil.

What you'll need:

•   An empty plastic water bottle
•   Uncooked rice
•   A pencil

Try it out:
1. Fill the plastic bottle to the top with uncooked rice. Once the bottle is filled all the way, then press the rice to compress it tightly.
2. Insert the pencil into the rice and press it down to the bottom of the bottle.
3. Lift the bottle by the pencil slowly. Note: Sometimes you have to adjust the pencil to make sure it is secure.
4. Once it is secure, you will be able to lift the bottle because the friction between the rice and pencil secures the pencil in place.

PAPER CLIP GRAVITY EXPERIMENT

Test the power of gravity with paper clips.

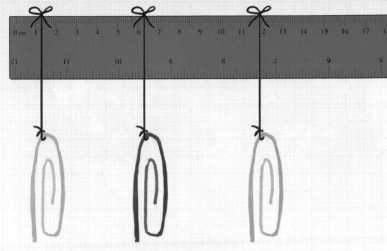

What you'll need:

- A ruler or yardstick
- 3 paper clips
- Yarn

Try it out:
1. Cut three 12" pieces of yarn.
2. Tie one end of each of the pieces of yarn to your ruler. Be sure to evenly space out the pieces.
3. Tie the other end of each piece of yarn to a paper clip.
4. Once all of your paper clips are attached to the yarn, hold your ruler up in front of you.
5. Tilt your ruler back and forth and left to right. Notice that even when the ruler is tilted, Earth's gravity still pulls the paper clips straight down toward the ground.

WATER BOTTLE GRAVITY EXPERIMENT

Learn about gravitational pull and weight using water bottles.

What you'll need:

- A stool
- Two unbreakable plastic water bottles

Try it out:
1. Fill one of your water bottles up about halfway with water (be sure the lid is secure) and leave the second water bottle empty.
2. Stand on top of the stool while holding both water bottles.
3. Hold the water bottles out in front of you so that they are both the same distance from the ground.
4. Drop the bottles. Notice how both water bottles hit the ground at the same time, even though the water bottle filled with water is heavier. Both bottles hit the ground at the same time because Earth's gravitational pull affects all objects regardless of their weight.

GLOSSARY

Acceleration – the change in an object's velocity over time

Displacement – the overall change in the position of an object; its ending position minus its starting position

Distance – the total amount of ground covered by a traveling object

Force – a push or pull exerted on an object that causes a change in that object's motion

Friction – a force between two objects that resists motion

Gravity – a force that causes all objects to be pulled toward each other

Inertia – the resistance of an object to change its current state of motion, for example: start, stop, turn, speed up, or slow down

Mass – the measurement of how much matter makes up an object

Matter – the substance that all material is made of

Newton's laws of motion – laws created by Sir Isaac Newton that explain how forces interact with objects

Physics – a branch of science that studies matter and its motion

Speed – the distance an object travels over time

Velocity – an object's displacement over time in a specific direction

more friction

less friction